BIBLE PUZZLERS

ALL ABOUT ANGELS

JIM EICHENBERGER

STANDARD PUBLISHING
Cincinnati, Ohio

In memory of my maternal grandmother, Lois Wallace, who always enjoyed a good puzzle.

All Scripture quotations, unless otherwise indicated, are taken from the HOLY BIBLE, NEW INTERNATIONAL VERSION®. NIV®. Copyright © 1973, 1978, 1984 by International Bible Society. Used by permission of Zondervan Publishing House. All rights reserved.

The Standard Publishing Company, Cincinnati, Ohio
A division of Standex International Corporation

©1997 by The Standard Publishing Company
All rights reserved
Printed in the United States of America

04 03 02 01 00 99 98 97   5 4 3 2 1

ISBN 0-7847-0588-7

Contents

Angels and the Greatest Story—Crossword 1	4
Angelic Mailboxes—Puzzle 1	6
Angels and God's Judgment—Puzzle 1	7
The Evil Angel—Angel Quotes #1	8
Angel Facts—Puzzles 1 & 2	10
Angelic Travel Agents—Puzzle 1	11
Angelic Mailboxes—Puzzle 2	12
Doing Their Duty—Puzzle 1	13
Angelic Birth Announcements—Puzzle 1	14
Angels to the Rescue—Cryptosearch 1	15
Angels and the Greatest Story—Crossword 2	16
Singing of Angels	18
Angelic Mailboxes—Puzzle 3	19
Angels and God's Judgment—Puzzle 2	20
Angel Quips	21
Angelic Travel Agents—Puzzle 2	22
Angelic Birth Announcements—Puzzle 2	23
Angels to the Rescue—Cryptosearch 2	24
Angelic Mailboxes—Puzzle 4	25
Angels and Men—Angel Quotes #2	26
Doing Their Duty—Puzzle 2	28
Angelic Birth Announcements—Puzzle 3	29
Doing Their Duty—Puzzle 3	30
Angelic Mailboxes—Puzzle 5	31
Angels and the Greatest Story—Crossword 3	32
Angels and God's Judgment—Puzzle 3	34
Angelic Birth Announcements—Puzzle 4	35
Angels to the Rescue—Cryptosearch 3	36
Angel Facts—Puzzles 3 & 4	37
Angelic Mailboxes—Puzzle 6	38
Angelic Travel Agents—Puzzle 3	39
Add 'em Up	40
Angels to the Rescue—Cryptosearch 4	41
Angels and God's Judgment—Puzzle 4	42
Angelic Mailboxes—Puzzle 7	43
Angels and the Greatest Story—Crossword 4	44
Answers	46

Angels and the Greatest Story
Crossword #1

Matthew 1:18-25

Across
1. Promised (v. 18)
6. Not apart (v. 18)
9. Virtuous (v. 19)
12. Word denoting one's identity (v. 21)
13. Wed (v. 18)
15. Became visible (v. 20)
17. Not loudly (v. 19)
18. Female spouse (v. 20)
19. Transgressions (v. 21)
20. Not separate (v. 18)
21. Fearful (v. 20)
23. You and me (v. 23)
25. Isaiah, for one (v. 22)
27. Caused conception (v. 20)
29. God with us (v. 23)
31. Lay open (v. 19)

Down
1. Not private (v. 19)
2. Shame (v. 19)
3. Sleeper's vision (v. 20)
4. Chaste woman (v. 23)
5. Namesake of Jacob's favorite son (v. 18)
7. Male spouse (v. 19)
8. Dissolve a marriage (v. 19)
10. Male child (v. 21)
11. Persons (v. 21)
14. Second king of Israel (v. 20)
16. The bearing of a child (v. 18)
22. Thought about (v. 20)
23. State of being joined (v. 25)
24. The Almighty (v. 23)
26. Emerged from sleep (v. 24)
28. Entitle (v. 23)
30. Master (v. 20)
32. Rescue (v. 21)

Angelic Mailboxes
Puzzle 1

Angels are messengers. The messages they bring are always from God and His Son, Jesus. In the book of Revelation we have messages from Jesus directed toward seven churches. To the angel of each church, a different description of Jesus is given.

Fit the boxes above into the grid below to reveal one of them.

© 1997 by The Standard Publishing Company.
Permission is granted to reproduce this page for ministry purposes only—not for resale.

Angels and God's Judgment
Puzzle 1

The Scripture verses listed tell of angels carrying out God's judgment on a person or persons. The words listed from these verses are hidden in the puzzle forward, backward, up, down, or diagonally.
When you have found all the hidden words, transfer the remaining letters, moving from left to right, to the blanks below. These letters will spell out an appropriate title for this Bible story.

```
S T A N D I N G K N
S A E S O P P O A E
E D H T A P P N E T
L N R N A E G N P A
K Y G A N R E L S E
C E D V Y R E E T B
E K B R U E Y K E A
R N E E O E N S L L
B O A S L W A I L A
A D E N N I S M V K
```

Numbers 22:21-35

VINEYARDS   DONKEY   SWORD
RECKLESS   OPPOSE   OPEN
SERVANTS   SINNED   EYES
STANDING   ANGRY   TELL
BEATEN   BALAK   PATH
SPEAK

__ __ __ __ __ __ __ __ __ __ __ __ __ __ __

__ __ __ __ __ __

The Evil Angel
Angel Quotes #1

Authors of classical literature often referred to angels. Complete this puzzle to reveal a quote about the prince of evil angels, Satan.

Fill in the answers to the clues. Then transfer the letters to the correspondingly numbered squares in the diagram.

1. Job's accuser (Job 1:6)

   __ __ __ __ __
   16 1 38 7 2

2. Devil's common disguise (2 Corinthians 11:14)

   __ __ __ __ __   __ __
   7 2 33 40 20   23 39

   __ __ __ __ __
   5 12 25 28 15

3. Patriarch of falsehood (John 8:44)

   __ __ __ __ __ __ of __ __ __ __
   39 1 21 14 9 31   41 18 4 37

4. To throw (Revelation 12:9)

   __ __ __ __
   34 24 8 19

5. Battle (Ephesians 6:12)

   __ __ __ __ __ __ __
   16 35 11 24 3 13 42 29

8   © 1997 by The Standard Publishing Company.
Permission is granted to reproduce this page for ministry purposes only—not for resale.

6. Place of eternal punishment (2 Peter 2:4)

   __ __ __ __
   22 4 42 20

7. To refuse to submit (James 4:7)

   __ __ __ __ __ __
   8 36 6 32 16 27

8. Sin gives _____ to death. (James 1:15)

   __ __ __ __ __
   30 12 31 17 26

9. To consume with fire

   __ __ __ __
   10 24 8 2

William Shakespeare, **Macbeth,** Act IV, Scene 3

Angel Facts
Puzzles 1 & 2

The letters in each vertical column go into the squares directly below them, but not necessarily in the order in which they appear. A black square indicates the end of a word. When you have placed all the letters in their correct squares, you will be able to read a fact about angels across the diagram from left to right.

Puzzle 1

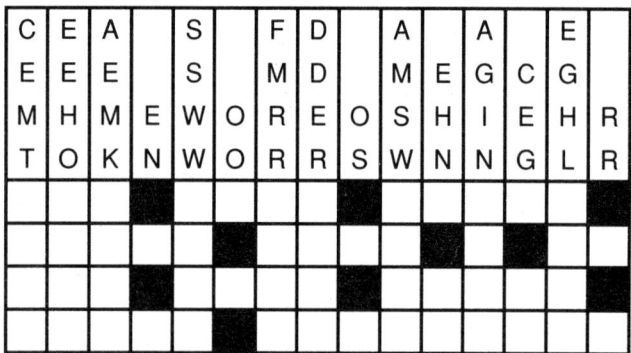

Puzzle 2

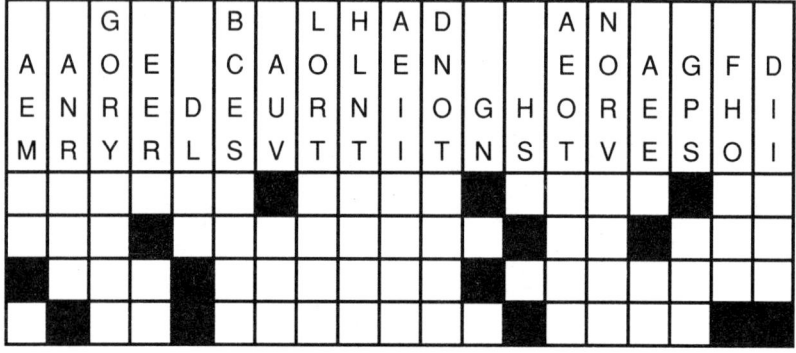

Angelic Travel Agents
Puzzle 1

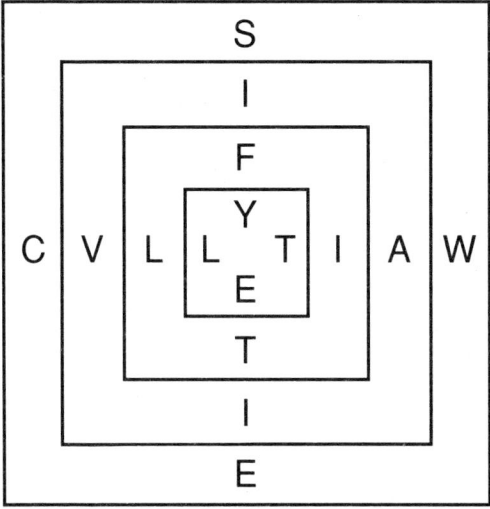

In the puzzle above, each square has four letters. Mentally "turn" each square so that four words are formed reading from outside to inside. Write those words below.

_____

_____

_____

_____

These words all relate to a specific Bible character whose travel was directed by angels. Who was it?

_____

© 1997 by The Standard Publishing Company.
Permission is granted to reproduce this page for ministry purposes only—not for resale.

Angelic Mailboxes
Puzzle 2

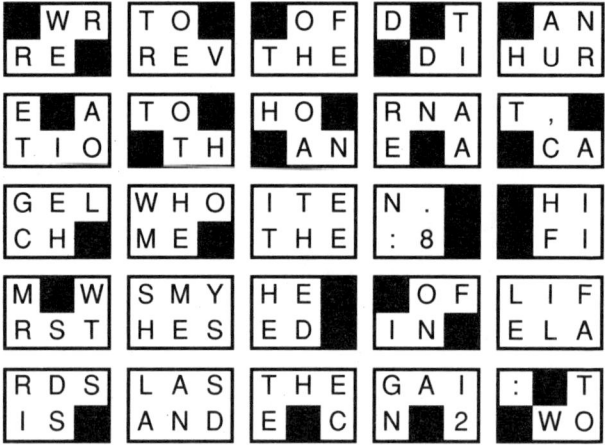

Angels are messengers. The messages they bring are always from God and His Son, Jesus. In the book of Revelation we have messages from Jesus directed toward seven churches. To the angel of each church, a different description of Jesus is given.
Fit the boxes above into the grid below to reveal one of them.

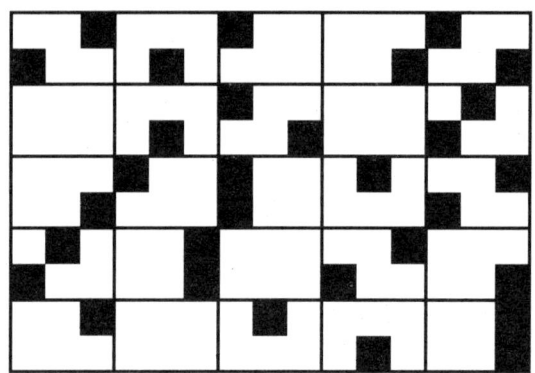

© 1997 by The Standard Publishing Company.
Permission is granted to reproduce this page for ministry purposes only—not for resale.

Doing Their Duty
Puzzle 1

Many duties of angels are described in the Bible. One of those duties is encoded below.

In the long-division problem, letters are substituted for numbers. Determine the value of each letter to make the problem work. Then arrange the letters in the spaces above it to decode the angelic duty.

(We have started the puzzle for you. D=3.)

$$\frac{G}{0} \ \frac{\_}{1} \ \frac{\_}{2} \ \frac{D}{3} \quad \frac{\_}{4} \ \frac{\_}{5} \ \frac{\_}{6} \ \frac{\_}{7} \ \frac{D}{3} \ \frac{\_}{2} \ \frac{\_}{8} \ \frac{\_}{9}$$

Matthew 18:10

```
                      I N
        3 ⌐ 3          3
  H I D E │ D E N I E D
          3 3
          D D E R E
                    3
          H A C U D
            H U L C R
                I I A
```

Angelic Birth Announcements
Puzzle 1

O	Q	H	F	T	S	M	Z	E
J	U	H	T	H	N	O	N	G
B	A	J	I	B	I	N	M	E
B	I	H	K	C	M	F	R	R
S	D	M	B	U	J	W	F	P
E	L	B	S	Z	U	D	N	O
K	D	F	B	A	S	J	F	M
Y	F	B	I	B	S	H	B	G
D	M	J	Y	B	A	D	S	I

In the grid above, choose the letter in the alphabet immediately before or after each letter to form clues to this puzzle. Write those clues below.

_ _ _ _ _ _ _ _ _ _ _ _ _ _

_ _ _ _ _ _ _ _

_ _ _

_ _ _ _ _ _ _ _ _

_ _ _ _ _ _ _ _ _ _ _ _ _ _

_ _ _ _ _ _

_ _ _ _ _ _ _

_ _ _ _ _ _ _ _ _

These words all relate to a specific Bible character whose birth was announced by angels. Who was it?

_____

Angels to the Rescue
Cryptosearch 1

Below is a passage of Scripture in a substitution code. GOD IS GOOD might become MRX DG MRRX if M is substituted for G, R for O, X for D, etc.
The underlined words in this passage, when decoded, can be found in the word search puzzle above. They are hidden in the puzzle forward, backward, up, down, or diagonally.
Work between the two puzzles to solve them both.

PMX <u>HZVXF</u> RA PMX <u>FRUG</u> <u>ARWZG</u> <u>MHVHU</u>

ZXHU H <u>ICUEZV</u> EZ PMX <u>GXIXUP</u>; EP KHI

PMX ICUEZV <u>PMHP</u> EI <u>SXIEGX</u> PMX <u>URHG</u> PR

<u>IMWU</u>. . . . <u>PMXZ</u> PMX HZVXF RA PMX FRUG

<u>PRFG</u> MXU, "VR <u>SHBT</u> PR <u>QRWU</u> <u>NEIPUXII</u>

HZG <u>IWSNEP</u> PR MXU."

Angels and the Greatest Story
Crossword #2

Luke 2:8-15

Across
1. Groups of sheep (v. 8)
3. Greek for Messiah (v. 11)
5. Radiated (v. 9)
6. Rescuer (v. 11)
8. Residing (v. 8)
10. The Deity (v.14)
12. Herdsmen (v. 8)
13. Assemblage (v. 13)
17. Infant (v. 12)
19. Worshipful praise (v. 14)
21. Feeding trough (v. 12)
23. Army (v. 13)
24. Same as 22 Down
25. Enfolded (v. 12)
27. Son of Jesse (v. 11)
29. Persons (v. 10)
30. At the zenith (v. 14)
31. Good will (v. 14)
32. Remains (v. 14)
33. Abruptly (v. 13)
34. City of David (v. 15)

Down
2. Retaining (v. 8)
4. Deeply afraid (v. 9)
5. Giving utterance (v. 13)
6. That which signifies (v. 12)
7. Pastures (v. 8)
9. Observe (v. 8)
11. In the vicinity (v. 8)
13. Textile pieces (v. 12)
14. Eventide (v. 8)
15. Prone (v. 12)
16. Gladness (v. 10)
18. Fearful (v. 10)
20. On this date (v. 11)
21. Male persons (v. 14)
22. Proceed (v. 15)
26. Our planet (v. 14)
28. Became visible (v. 9)
30. Belonging to him (v. 14)
33. Employ vision (v. 15)

© 1997 by The Standard Publishing Company.
Permission is granted to reproduce this page for ministry purposes only—not for resale.

Singing of Angels

Many hymns refer to angels. Match the following song titles with the phrase taken from their first verses.

Song Title

___ 1. **Hark, the Herald Angels Sing**
___ 2. **Praise Him! Praise Him!**
___ 3. **While Shepherds Watched Their Flocks**
___ 4. **All Hail the Power of Jesus' Name!**
___ 5. **The First Noel**
___ 6. **Christ the Lord Is Risen Today**
___ 7. **It Came Upon the Midnight Clear**
___ 8. **What Child Is This?**
___ 9. **Tell Me the Story of Jesus**
___10. **O Come, All Ye Faithful**

Phrase from first verse

A. "Tell how the angels, in chorus..."
B. "The angel of the Lord came down..."
C. "From angels bending near the earth..."
D. "Born the King of angels."
E. "With th' angelic host proclaim..."
F. "...highest archangels in glory..."
G. "...the angel did say..."
H. "Let angels prostrate fall..."
I. "Sons of men and angels say..."
J. "Whom angels greet with anthems sweet..."

Angelic Mailboxes
Puzzle 3

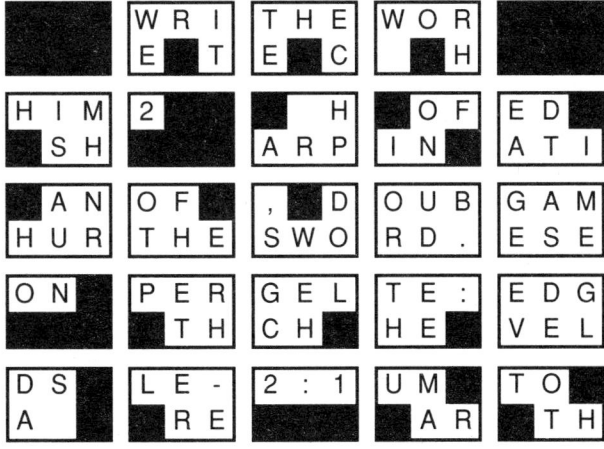

Angels are messengers. The messages they bring are always from God and His Son, Jesus. In the book of Revelation we have messages from Jesus directed toward seven churches. To the angel of each church, a different description of Jesus is given.

Fit the boxes above into the grid below to reveal one of them.

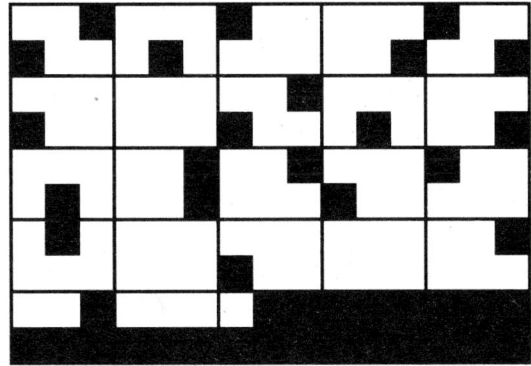

© 1997 by The Standard Publishing Company.
Permission is granted to reproduce this page for ministry purposes only—not for resale.

Angels and God's Judgment
Puzzle 2

The Scripture verses listed tell of angels carrying out God's judgment on a person or persons. The words listed from these verses are hidden in the puzzle forward, backward, up, down, or diagonally.

When you have found all the hidden words, transfer the remaining letters, moving from left to right, to the blanks below. These letters will spell out an appropriate title for this Bible story.

```
A  E  R  A  S  E  A  C  Q  S
E  P  H  B  L  A  S  T  U  S
D  E  E  S  R  N  E  T  A  E
U  A  O  Y  M  D  D  I  R  R
J  C  R  L  S  R  O  R  R  D
N  E  O  P  S  T  O  R  E  D
O  U  Y  P  C  B  F  W  L  A
D  K  A  U  E  D  G  N  I  K
I  O  L  S  E  R  V  A  N  T
S  W  P  U  B  L  I  C  G  N
```

Acts 12:19-24

QUARRELING   SUPPLY   SIDON
CAESAREA   EATEN   WORMS
ADDRESS   JUDEA   KING
BLASTUS   PEACE   FOOD
SERVANT   ROYAL
PUBLIC   ROBES

_ _ _ _ _ _ _ _ _ _ _ _ _ _ _

_ _ _ _ _

Angel Quips

Each of the following is a pun about angels in a substitution code. The code is different for each quip. Single letters, and 2-letter and 3-letter words are a good place to start. The Scripture reference may provide some clues. Additional clues are found at the bottom of the page.

1. IN DEN AZEN BYDB CDXFNW

   IDAX'B "WFGX" DVGZB BYN

   DXHNW BYDB ADMNC YFK!

   Daniel 6:22

2. ESY TAJYMO KSROY ATLYO KY

   HARK TXY LQBSTYM TAC

   JTDXQYM—ARE "SYXTMC!"

   Jude 9; Luke 1:26

3. RUN PI U "FLI" LS IALXKFO SLA

   UZYOFN IL NUHO U SUTPFE

   SALT   NLJLT?

   Genesis 19:15

Quip 1: DEN represents ARE.
Quip 2: HARK represents KNOW.
Quip 3: SALT represents FROM.

Angelic Travel Agents
Puzzle 2

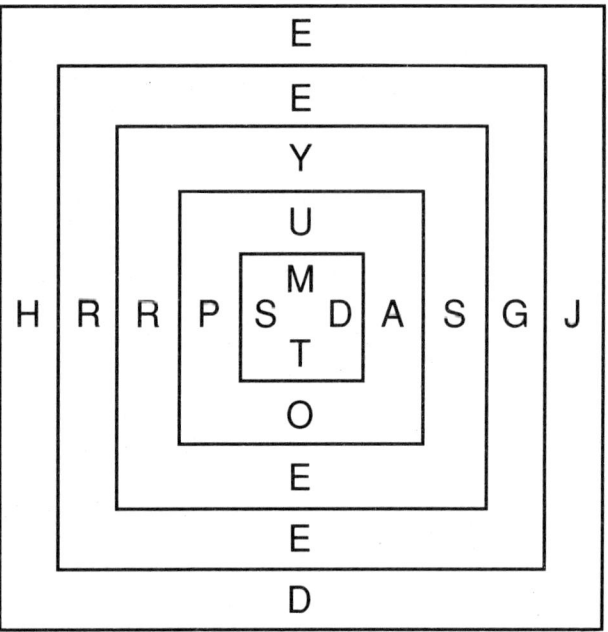

In the puzzle above, each square has four letters. Mentally "turn" each square so that four words are formed reading from outside to inside. Write those words below.

_____

_____

_____

_____

These words all relate to a specific Bible character whose travel was directed by angels. Who was it?

_____

Angelic Birth Announcements
Puzzle 2

O	B	Y	B	Q	D	S	I	G
N	X	X	J	K	M	S	I	H
R	A	F	E	B	W	P	S	V
J	U	G	H	N	E	L	H	M
F	C	N	N	X	H	M	M	M
D	U	F	S	D	O	E	S	I
Q	P	O	D	N	E	E	B	W
J	C	U	H	Q	H	H	O	L
B	S	Z	K	N	R	F	O	G

In the grid above, choose the letter in the alphabet immediately before or after each letter to form clues to this puzzle. Write those clues below.

_ _ _ _ _ _ _

_ _ _   _ _ _ _   _ _ _ _   _ _ ?

_ _ _ _ _   _ _ _ _   _ _ _

_ _ _ _ _ _ _   _ _ _ _ _   _ _ _ _ _ _   _ _ _ _

_ _ _ _ _ _ _   _ _   _ _ _ _ _

_ _ _ _ _ _

_ _ _ _

_ _ _ _ _ _

These words all relate to a specific Bible character whose birth was announced by angels. Who was it?

_____

© 1997 by The Standard Publishing Company.
Permission is granted to reproduce this page for ministry purposes only—not for resale.

Angels to the Rescue
Cryptosearch 2

O	F	D	E	I	L	P	E	R	X
R	R	N	I	R	W	S	M	A	K
U	O	E	F	A	U	F	N	N	J
O	M	V	E	A	S	Y	O	G	C
Y	G	A	C	D	T	W	B	E	A
D	L	E	H	H	T	I	W	L	X
I	B	H	I	A	D	H	K	J	H
H	A	N	D	L	R	A	E	F	A
Y	G	Y	L	N	O	B	U	R	V
W	J	K	D	E	L	L	A	C	E

Below is a passage of Scripture in a substitution code. GOD IS GOOD might become MRX DG MRRX if M is substituted for G, R for O, X for D, etc.

The underlined words in this passage, when decoded, can be found in the word search puzzle above. They are hidden in the puzzle forward, backward, up, down, or diagonally.

Work between the two puzzles to solve them both.

A O K   K E W   <u>M H R W B</u>   X G   K E W   <u>B X Z Q</u>   <u>D M B B W Q</u>

X O K   K X   E T I   <u>G Z X I</u>   E W M N W H ,   "<u>M A Z M E M I</u>!

M A Z M E M I !"   "<u>E W Z W</u>   T   M I ,"   E W   <u>Z W J B T W Q</u> .

"Q X   H X K   B M V   M   <u>E M H Q</u>   X H   K E W   A X V ,"   E W

<u>C M T Q</u> .   "Q X   H X K   Q X   <u>M H V K E T H R</u>   K X   E T I .   H X F

T   <u>U H X F</u>   K E M K   V X O   <u>G W M Z</u>   R X Q ,   <u>A W D M O C W</u>

V X O   <u>E M N W</u>   H X K   <u>F T K E E W B Q</u>   G Z X I   I W   <u>V X O Z</u>

C X H ,   V X O Z   <u>X H B V</u>   C X H . "

© 1997 by The Standard Publishing Company.
Permission is granted to reproduce this page for ministry purposes only—not for resale.

Angelic Mailboxes
Puzzle 4

Angels are messengers. The messages they bring are always from God and His Son, Jesus. In the book of Revelation we have messages from Jesus directed toward seven churches. To the angel of each church, a different description of Jesus is given.
Fit the boxes above into the grid below to reveal one of them.

Angels and Men
Angel Quotes #2

Authors of classical literature often referred to angels. Complete this puzzle to reveal a quote comparing angels and men.

Fill in the answers to the clues. Then transfer the letters to the correspondingly numbered squares in the diagram.

1. Man's rank when compared to angels (Psalm 8:5).

   ___ ___ ___ ___ ___
   7   2   15 27 33

2. To receive a bequest; Angels serve those who will _____ salvation (Hebrews 1:14).

   ___ ___ ___ ___ ___ ___ ___
   13 14 12 17 3   13 32

3. Extremely fearful (as when encountering angels) (Daniel 8:17).

   ___ ___ ___ ___ ___ ___ ___ ___ ___
   30 34 9   29 13 1   13 19 36

4. Express divine reverence—Men must not do this to angels (Colossians 2:18).

   ___ ___ ___ ___ ___ ___ _P_
   15 5   33 25 12 13

5. Men will do this to angels (1 Corinthians 6:3).

   _J_ ___ ___ ___ ___
       10 36 22 23

6. "He will command his angels . . . so that you will not strike your _____ against a _____" (Psalm 91:11, 12).

   __ __ __ __   __ __ __ __ __
   4 2 31 32   11 30 6 21 27

7. "But many who are _____ will be _____" (Matthew 19:30).

   __ __ __ __ __   __ __ __ __
   26 13 18 8 32   24 20 25 30

8. Mother of Ishmael (Genesis 21:17)

   __ __ __ __ __
   16 28 22 35 29

Alexander Pope, **Essay on Criticism,** Part III

Doing Their Duty
Puzzle 2

Many duties of angels are described in the Bible. One of those duties is encoded below.

In the long-division problem, letters are substituted for numbers. Determine the value of each letter to make the problem work. Then arrange the letters in the spaces above it to decode the angelic duty.

```
    F _ _ _ _       A _ _ _ _
    0 1 2 3 4       5 6 7 8 9
         2 Kings 19:35
```

```
                  U T T E R
        H U G ) T R U S T E E
                H U G
                ─────
                U H S S
                U G T E
                ─────
                  U R U T
                  U G T E
                  ─────
                    G M M E
                    G T S M
                    ─────
                      U I G E
                      U R M O
                      ─────
                        U M E
```

28

Angelic Birth Announcements
Puzzle 3

In the grid above, choose the letter in the alphabet immediately before or after each letter to form clues to this puzzle. Write those clues below.

__ __ __ __ __

__ __ __ __

__ __ __ __ __ __ __

__ __ __ __   __ __ __ __   __ __ __ __ __ __ __ __ __ __

__ __ __ __ __ __ __ __

__ __ __ __ __   __ __   __ __ __ __

__ __   __ __ __ __ __ __   __ __ __   __ __   __ __ __ __

__ __   __ __ __   __ __ __ __

These words all relate to a specific Bible character whose birth was announced by angels. Who was it?

_____

Doing Their Duty
Puzzle 3

Many duties of angels are described in the Bible. One of those duties is encoded below.

In the long-division problem, letters are substituted for numbers. Determine the value of each letter to make the problem work. Then arrange the letters in the spaces above it to decode the angelic duty.

$\overline{0}\ \overline{1}\ \overline{2}\ \overline{3}\ \overline{4}\ \overline{5}\quad \overline{3}\ \overline{6}\ \overline{7}\quad \overline{4}\ \overline{8}\ \overline{4}\ \overline{9}\ \overline{2}$

Matthew 24:31

```
                    T H E
          ┌─────────────────
H A I L   │ S E A R C H
            I H H I
            ─────────
            A G S C C
              C R G E
              ─────────
              A T C R H
              A T I S T
              ─────────
                T L A
```

Angelic Mailboxes
Puzzle 5

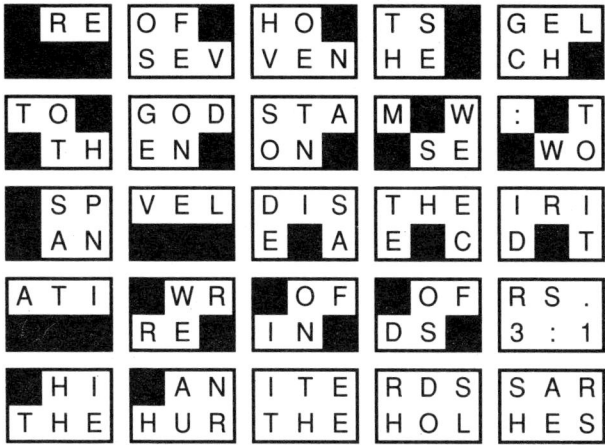

Angels are messengers. The messages they bring are always from God and His Son, Jesus. In the book of Revelation we have messages from Jesus directed toward seven churches. To the angel of each church, a different description of Jesus is given.
Fit the boxes above into the grid below to reveal one of them.

Angels and the Greatest Story
Crossword #3

Luke 22:39-46

Across
1. Our Savior (v. 39)
7. Enticement (v. 40)
9. Got up (v. 45)
10. Preposition indicating entry (v. 40)
12. Not her (v. 43)
14. Made stronger (v. 43)
16. Heavenly messenger (v. 43)
17. Spanish for "yes"
18. Sincerely (v. 44)
21. Spoke to God (v. 41)
23. Drinking vessel (v. 42)
25. Farther from (v. 41)
28. Not you (v. 42)
29. Surface of the earth (v. 44)
30. Spoke (v. 40)
33. Discovered (v. 45)
36. Very tired (v. 45)
38. Nevertheless (v. 42)
39. Not in (v. 39)
40. Trailed behind (v. 39)

Down
2. Grief (v. 45)
3. Of a rock (v. 41)
4. Descending, pulled by gravitation (v. 44)
5. Inclined to respond (v. 42)
6. Genuflected (v. 41)
8. Rushmore, for one (v. 39)
11. Green or black fruits (v. 39)
12. Abode of God (v. 43)
13. In dreamland (v. 45)
15. Followers (v. 39)
19. Arriving at (v. 40)
20. Went ___, returned (v. 45)
22. Red body fluid (v. 44)
24. Distress (v. 44)
25. Having existence (v. 44)
26. Not mine (v. 42)
27. Spherical masses of fluid (v. 44)
31. Conditional conjunction (v. 42)
32. Completed (v. 42)
34. Past tense of "go" (v. 45)
35. For what cause? (v. 46)
37. Accordant to habit (v. 39)

Angels and God's Judgment
Puzzle 3

The Scripture verses listed tell of angels carrying out God's judgment on a person or persons. The words listed from these verses are hidden in the puzzle forward, backward, up, down, or diagonally.

When you have found all the hidden words, transfer the remaining letters, moving from left to right, to the blanks below. These letters will spell out an appropriate title for this Bible story.

```
J M U D L E G N A G S
N O D D A H R A S E H
I R H E V E N I N M A
S N E N T O F N S E R
R I N N A C A I B H E
O N E R I C T G O B Z
C G A D H A N H D D E
H T H E R E A T I S R
A D R A M M E L E C H
S I R T D R O W S Y R
B A I H A N C A M P S
```

2 Kings 19:35-37

SENNACHERIB   NISROCH   NIGHT
ADRAMMELECH   ARARAT   ANGEL
ESARHADDON   MORNING   DEATH
SHAREZER   BODIES   CAMP
NINEVEH   SWORD

__ __ __ __ __ __ __ __ __ __

__ __ __ __ __ __ __ __ __ __ __ __ __ __

__ __ __ __ __ __ __ __ __ __ __ __

© 1997 by The Standard Publishing Company.
Permission is granted to reproduce this page for ministry purposes only—not for resale.

Angelic Birth Announcements
Puzzle 4

H	S	D	B	S	U	Q	D	F
T	N	G	N	B	L	Q	D	X
D	M	K	B	E	U	B	O	B
D	E	J	M	X	F	B	Q	T
H	R	B	M	Z	S	I	H	O
F	S	P	P	I	B	S	C	E
P	Q	U	G	F	K	N	S	E
M	B	T	F	G	R	R	B	S
B	I	B	A	S	B	I	B	L

In the grid above, choose the letter in the alphabet immediately before or after each letter to form clues to this puzzle. Write those clues below.

____ _____ __ _____

____ _____ __ _____

__ _____ ___ ____

___ ___ ____?

_____

_____

_____

These words all relate to a specific Bible character whose birth was announced by angels. Who was it?

_____

© 1997 by The Standard Publishing Company.
Permission is granted to reproduce this page for ministry purposes only—not for resale.

Angels to the Rescue
Cryptosearch 3

```
V Y P K U A S L S N S D
A S T N K B F O R T Y I
V X E R W O T A H T M A
Y T A C A A N G O K N S
L F O F O V I C Q G O Y
P J O U R N E Y E L C A
Y U E O C A D L I E S D
T B M X D H I F E M I T
U H A J I L E D W D P U
B A C K N A R D R O L N
```

Below is a passage of Scripture in a substitution code. GOD IS GOOD might become MRX DG MRRX if M is substituted for G, R for O, X for D, etc.

The underlined words in this passage, when decoded, can be found in the word search puzzle above. They are hidden in the puzzle forward, backward, up, down, or diagonally.

Work between the two puzzles to solve them both.

VXTAIO QIH IBMITS IPS MIP BRM OTH XTBV. IXX IU RPFV IP IPNVX URWFOVS OTG IPS HITS, "NVU WC IPS VIU." UOV IPNVX RB UOV XRMS FIGV ZIFJ I HVFRPS UTGV IPS URWFOVS OTG IPS HITS, "NVU WC IPS VIU, BRM UOV ARWMPVD TH URR GWFO BRM DRW." HR OV NRU WC IPS IUV IPS SMIPJ. HUMVPN-UOVPVS ZD UOIU BRRS, OV UMIEVXVS BRMUD SIDH IPS PTNOUH.

36   © 1997 by The Standard Publishing Company.
Permission is granted to reproduce this page for ministry purposes only—not for resale.

Angel Facts
Puzzles 3 & 4

The letters in each vertical column go into the squares directly below them, but not necessarily in the order in which they appear. A black square indicates the end of a word. When you have placed all the letters in their correct squares, you will be able to read a fact about angels across the diagram from left to right.

Puzzle 3

A	E	A					A	A		O	E	
A	N	A	D	B	H	C	A	E		I	O	I	P
D	R	G	E	E	S	T	M	E	N	E	N	P	N	R
I	T	S	T	L	U	U	R	R	R	T	S	S	T	S

Puzzle 4

M		E	C			B	F				F	E		A	A		I	E		
N	A	N	H	E		O	N	K	I		H	E	E	B	A	B	L	E		A
O	G	R	L	E		O	O	L	S	N	R	O	L	I	I	B	L	F		I
S	U	T	Y	S	B	O	U	T	Y	T	S	P	R	M	K	T	O	O	N	S

© 1997 by The Standard Publishing Company.
Permission is granted to reproduce this page for ministry purposes only—not for resale.

Angelic Mailboxes
Puzzle 6

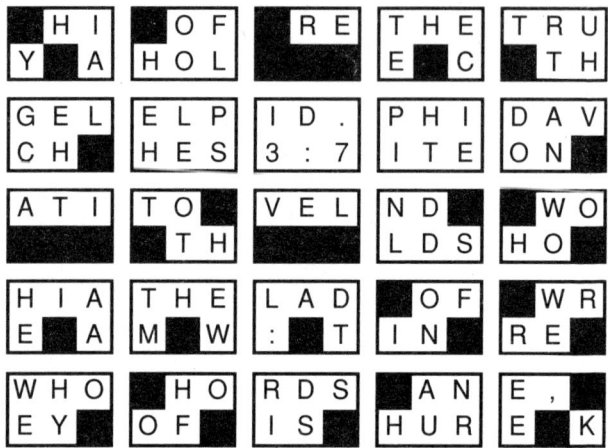

Angels are messengers. The messages they bring are always from God and His Son, Jesus. In the book of Revelation we have messages from Jesus directed toward seven churches. To the angel of each church, a different description of Jesus is given.

Fit the boxes above into the grid below to reveal one of them.

Angelic Travel Agents
Puzzle 3

In the puzzle below, each square has four letters. Mentally "turn" each square so that four words are formed reading from outside to inside. Write those words below.

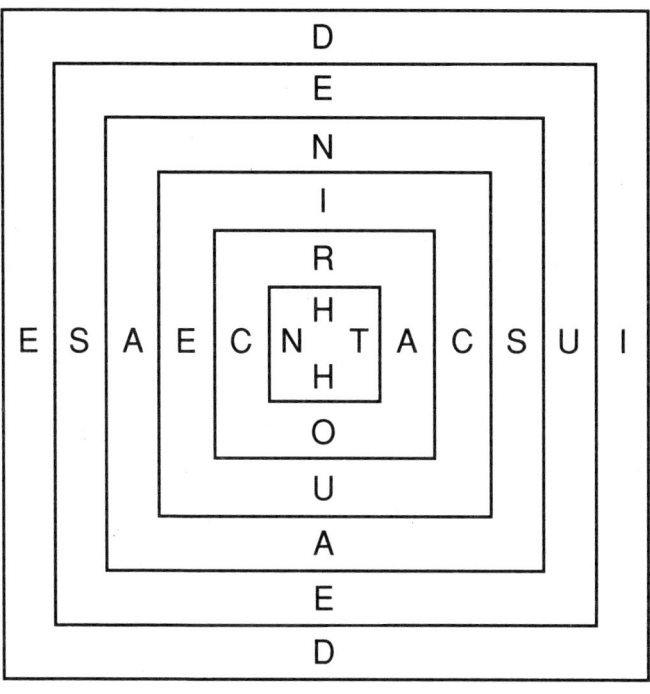

These words all relate to a specific Bible character whose travel was directed by angels. Who was it?

_____

Add 'em Up

Many names and descriptions of angels are given in the Bible. Some of these are listed below.
Complete the names by identifying their missing letters. Each of the letters of the alphabet has been given a numerical value. These values can be found in the box below. If you subtract the sum of the given letters, you will know the sum of the missing letters.

A	B	C	D	E	F	G	H	I	J	K	L	M
1	2	3	4	5	6	7	8	9	10	11	12	13
N	O	P	Q	R	S	T	U	V	W	X	Y	Z
14	15	16	17	18	19	20	21	22	23	24	25	26

1. M+_+G+H+T+_ +O+_+_+S=135 Psalm 103:20

2. H+_+_V+_+_+L+Y +H+_+_+T+S=173 Psalm 103:21

3. C+_+_+R+_+_+_+S +O+F +_+I+R+_=152 2 Kings 6:17

4. _+_+L+Y +O+N+_+_=113 Daniel 4:17

5. _+E+A+_+E+_+L+Y +_+_+I+N+G+_=148 Psalm 89:6

6. M+_+R+_+_+N+G +_+_+_+R+S=167 Job 38:7

7. G+_+_+R+D+_+_+N +_+_+E+_+U+B=132 Ezekiel 28:14

8. S+_+_+_+P+H+S=86 Isaiah 6:2

9. _+_+V+_+N+G +_+R+_+_+T+_+R+_+S=183 Revelation 4:6

10. M+_+_+_+E+_+G+_+R=105 Daniel 4:13

40   © 1997 by The Standard Publishing Company.
      Permission is granted to reproduce this page for ministry purposes only—not for resale.

Angels to the Rescue
Cryptosearch 4

N	E	K	N	I	H	T	E	D	O
A	Q	R	J	V	W	P	I	D	S
H	E	V	O	E	S	A	I	R	W
T	O	C	L	M	S	S	E	A	O
L	C	V	N	A	P	U	J	W	R
L	E	G	I	O	N	S	S	E	D
I	L	O	S	Y	H	G	J	I
W	C	A	N	N	O	T	E	Y	X
P	L	A	C	E	A	U	S	L	H
K	C	A	B	F	M	Z	R	K	S

Below is a passage of Scripture in a substitution code. GOD IS GOOD might become MRX DG MRRX if M is substituted for G, R for O, X for D, etc.
The underlined words in this passage, when decoded, can be found in the word search puzzle above. They are hidden in the puzzle forward, backward, up, down, or diagonally.
Work between the two puzzles to solve them both.

"VLW <u>IJLU</u> <u>AOJUM</u> <u>TCFN</u> YG YWA <u>VZCFK</u>,"

<u>SKALA</u> <u>ACYM</u> WJ BYP, "XJU CZZ OBJ <u>MUCO</u>

WBK AOJUM <u>OYZZ</u> MYK TI WBK AOJUM. MJ

IJL <u>WBYGN</u> Y <u>FCGGJW</u> <u>FCZZ</u> JG PI <u>XCWBKU</u>,

CGM BK OYZZ CW <u>JGFK</u> VLW CW PI <u>MYAV-</u>

<u>JACZ</u> <u>PJUK</u> <u>WBCG</u> <u>WOKZEK</u> ZKQYJGA JX

<u>CGQKZA</u>?"

Angels and God's Judgment
Puzzle 4

The Scripture verses listed tell of angels carrying out God's judgment on a person or persons. The words listed from these verses are hidden in the puzzle forward, backward, up, down, or diagonally.
When you have found all the hidden words, transfer the remaining letters, moving from left to right, to the blanks below. These letters will spell out an appropriate title for this Bible story.

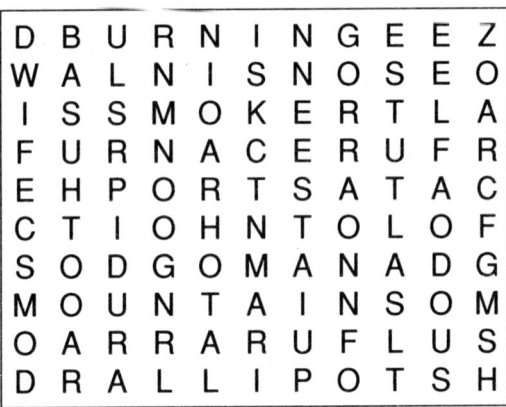

Genesis 19:1-29

CATASTROPHE	FURNACE	SALT
DAUGHTERS	PILLAR	STOP
MOUNTAINS	SULFUR	WIFE
SONS-IN-LAW	SMOKE	ZOAR
BURNING	FLEE	LOT

___ ___ ___ ___ ___ ___ ___ ___ ___ ___ ___

___ ___ ___ ___ ___ ___ ___ ___ ___ ___ ___ ___ ___ ___

Angelic Mailboxes
Puzzle 7

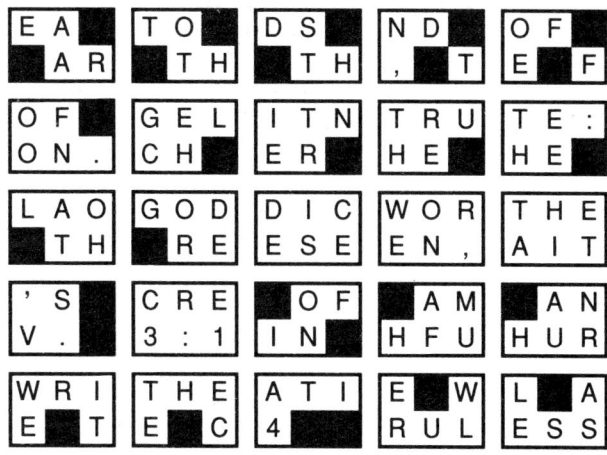

Angels are messengers. The messages they bring are always from God and His Son, Jesus. In the book of Revelation we have messages from Jesus directed toward seven churches. To the angel of each church, a different description of Jesus is given.
Fit the boxes above into the grid below to reveal one of them.

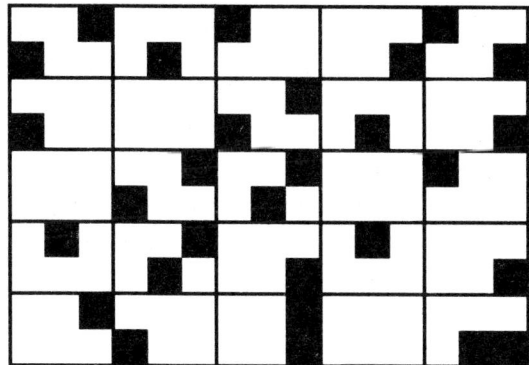

Angels and the Greatest Story
Crossword #4

Matthew 28:1-10

Across
1. God's dwelling (v. 2)
3. Sentries (v. 4)
5. Vault for the dead (v. 1)
7. Seismic disturbance (v. 2)
10. Employ vision (v. 6)
11. *Anno Domini* (abbr.)
12. Came together with (v. 9)
14. Approach (v. 6)
16. Abruptly (v. 9)
19. To another location (v. 8)
20. Fearful (v. 4)
22. Consumed with (v. 8)
23. Salutations (v. 9)
25. Alabaster (v. 3)
26. Held (v. 9)
28. Followers (v. 8)
30. Male siblings (v. 10)
34. Gladness (v. 8)
35. Revered (v. 9)

Down
1. Rushed (v. 8)
2. Having extreme force (v. 2)
3. Leave (v. 7)
4. Semblance (v. 3)
6. Not living (v. 4)
8. Ascended (v. 6)
9. With haste (v. 7)
10. Day of rest (v. 1)
13. Executed on a cross (v. 5)
15. From Magdala (v. 1)
17. Was prostrate (v. 6)
18. North of Judea (v. 7)
21. Not second (v. 1)
24. Moved by turning over (v. 2)
27. Bottoms of legs (v. 9)
29. Winter precipitation (v. 3)
31. Rock (v. 2)
32. Sunrise (v. 1)
33. Mother of Jesus (v. 1)

Answers

Angels and the Greatest Story—Crossword 1
Across: 1. pledged, 6. together, 9. righteous, 12. name, 13. married, 15. appeared, 17. quietly, 18. wife, 19. sins, 20. with, 21. afraid, 23. us, 25. prophet, 27. conceived, 29. Immanuel, 31. expose, **Down:** 1. public, 2. disgrace, 3. dream, 4. virgin, 5. Joseph, 7. husband, 8. divorce, 10. son, 11. people, 14. David, 16. birth, 22. considered, 23. union, 24. God, 26. woke, 28. call, 30. Lord, 32. save

Angelic Mailboxes—Puzzle 1
To the angel of the church in Ephesus write: These are the words of him who holds the seven stars in his right hand and walks among the seven . . . lampstands. Revelation 2:1

Angels and God's Judgment—Puzzle 1
An Angel Rebukes Balaam

The Evil Angel—Angel Quotes #1
1. Satan, 2. angel of light, 3. father of lies, 4. hurl, 5. struggle, 6. hell, 7. resist, 8. birth, 9. burn, "Angels are bright still though the brightest fell."

Angel Facts
Puzzle 1: The word angel comes from a Greek word which means messenger.
Puzzle 2: Angels that have fiery devotion to God are called "seraphim" or "burning ones."

Angelic Travel Agents—Puzzle 1
LOT was told by angels to flee the **evil city** of Sodom. His **wife** looked back and was turned into a pillar of **salt**. Genesis 19:16-26

Angelic Mailboxes—Puzzle 2
To the angel of the church in Smyrna write: These are the words of him who is the First and the Last, who died and came to life again. Revelation 2:8

Doing Their Duty—Puzzle 1
Guard Children

Angelic Birth Announcements—Puzzle 1
priestly division of Abijah, old, childless, relative of Mary, temple, Gabriel, Zechariah, Elizabeth. John the Baptist (Luke 1:5-25)

Angels to the Rescue—Cryptosearch 1
The angel of the Lord found Hagar near a spring in the desert; it was the spring that is beside the road to Shur. Then the angel of the Lord told her, "Go back to your mistress and submit to her." (Genesis 16:7, 9)

Angels and the Greatest Story—Crossword 2
Across: 1. flocks, 3. Christ, 5. shone, 6. Savior, 8. living, 10. God, 12. shepherds, 13. company, 17. baby, 19. glory, 21. manger, 23. host, 24. go, 25. wrapped, 27. David, 29. people, 30. highest, 31. favor, 32. rests, 33. suddenly, 34. Bethlehem, **Down:** 2. keeping, 4. terrified, 5. saying, 6. sign, 7. fields, 9. watch, 11. nearby, 13. cloths, 14. night, 15. lying, 16. joy, 18. afraid, 20. today, 21. men, 22. go, 26. earth, 28. appeared, 30. his, 33. see

Singing of Angels
1. E, 2. F, 3. B, 4. H, 5. G, 6. I, 7. C, 8. J, 9. A, 10. D

Angelic Mailboxes—Puzzle 3
To the angel of the church in Pergamum write: These are the words of him who has the sharp, double-edged sword. Revelation 2:12

Angels and God's Judgment—Puzzle 2
Herod is struck down.

Angel Quips
1. We are sure that Daniel wasn't "lion" about the angel that saved him!, 2. The angels whose names we know are Michael and Gabriel—not "Herald!", 3. Was it a "Lot" of trouble for angels to save a family from Sodom?

Angelic Travel Agents—Puzzle 2
An angel warned **JOSEPH** in a **dream** to take **Jesus** and Mary to **Egypt** to flee the wrath of **Herod.** Matthew 2:13

Angelic Birth Announcements—Puzzle 2
Nazareth, How will this be, favor with God, kingdom will never end, throne of David, virgin, Mary, Joseph. Jesus Christ (Luke 1:26-38)

Angels to the Rescue—Cryptosearch 2
But the angel of the LORD called out to him from heaven, "Abraham! Abraham!" "Here I am," he replied. "Do not lay a hand on the boy," he said. "Do not do anything to him. Now I know that you fear God, because you have not withheld from me your son, your only son." (Genesis 22:11, 12)

Angelic Mailboxes—Puzzle 4
To the angel of the church in Thyatira write: These are the words of the son of God, whose eyes are like blazing fire and whose feet are like burnished bronze. Revelation 2:18

Angels and Men—Angel Quotes #2
1. lower, 2. inherit, 3. terrified, 4. worship, 5. judge, 6. foot, stone, 7. first, last, 8. Hagar, "For fools rush in where angels fear to tread."

Doing Their Duty—Puzzle 2
Fought Armies

Angelic Birth Announcements—Puzzle 3
Manoah, Zorah, Danites, free from Philistines, Nazirite, drink no wine, no razor may be used on his head. Samson (Judges 13:1-25)

Doing Their Duty—Puzzle 3
Gather His Elect

Angelic Mailboxes—Puzzle 5
To the angel of the church in Sardis write: These are the words of him who holds the seven spirits of God and the seven stars. Revelation 3:1

Angels and the Greatest Story—Crossword 3
Across: 1. Jesus, 7. temptation, 9. rose, 10. into, 12. him, 14. strengthened, 16. angel, 17. si, 18. earnestly, 21. prayed, 23. cup, 25. beyond, 28. me, 29. ground, 30. said, 33. found, 36. exhausted, 38. yet, 39. out, 40. followed, **Down:** 2. sorrow, 3. stone's, 4. falling, 5. willing, 6. knelt, 8. mount, 11. olives, 12. Heaven, 13. asleep, 15. disciples, 19. reaching, 20. back, 22. blood, 24. anguish,

25. being, 26. yours, 27. drops, 31. if, 32. done, 34. went, 35. why, 37. usual

Angels and God's Judgment—Puzzle 3
Judgment of Sennacherib and the Assyrians

Angelic Birth Announcements—Puzzle 4
great trees of Mamre, well advanced in years, Is anything too hard for the LORD?, laughs, Sarah, Abraham. Isaac (Genesis 18:1-15)

Angels to the Rescue—Cryptosearch 3
Elijah was afraid and ran for his life. . . . All at once an angel touched him and said, "Get up and eat." . . . The angel of the LORD came back a second time and touched him and said, "Get up and eat, for the journey is too much for you." So he got up and ate and drank. Strengthened by that food, he traveled forty days and . . . nights. (1 Kings 19:3, 5, 7, 8)

Angel Facts
Puzzle 3: Angels are not dead human spirits, but are separate creations.
Puzzle 4: Many books speak of angels, but the Bible is the only reliable source of information.

Angelic Mailboxes—Puzzle 6
To the angel of the church in Philadelphia write: These are the words of him who is holy and true, who holds the key of David. Revelation 3:7

Angelic Travel Agents—Puzzle 3
PHILIP the **deacon** was sent to the **desert** road to teach an Ethiopian **eunuch** who was reading from the prophet **Isaiah.** Acts 8:26-39

Add 'em Up
1. mighty ones, 2. heavenly hosts, 3. chariots of fire, 4. holy ones, 5. heavenly beings, 6. morning stars, 7. guardian cherub, 8. seraphs, 9. living creatures, 10. messenger

Angels to the Rescue—Cryptosearch 4
"Put your sword back in its place," Jesus said to him. "For all who draw the sword will die by the sword. Do you think I cannot call on my Father, and he will at once put at my disposal more than twelve legions of angels?" (Matthew 26:52, 53)

Angels and God's Judgment—Puzzle 4
Destruction of Sodom and Gomorrah

Angelic Mailboxes—Puzzle 7
To the angel of the church in Laodicea write: These are the words of the Amen, the faithful and true witness, the ruler of God's creation. Revelation 3:14

Angels and the Greatest Story—Crossword 4
Across: 1. heaven, 3. guards, 5. tomb, 7. earthquake, 10. see, 11. AD, 12. met, 14. come, 16. suddenly, 19. away, 20. afraid, 22. filled, 23. greetings, 25. white, 26. clasped, 28. disciples, 30. brothers, 34. joy, 35. worshiped, **Down:** 1. hurried, 2. violent, 3. go, 4. appearance, 6. dead, 8. risen, 9. quickly, 10. Sabbath, 13. crucified, 15. Magdalene, 17. lay, 18. Galilee, 21. first, 24. rolled, 27. feet, 29. snow, 31. stone, 32. dawn, 33. Mary